Timmy Tries

Written by Mary K. Hawley
Illustrated by Melanie Hall

Celebration Press
An Imprint of Addison-Wesley
Educational Publishers, Inc.

Molly flies a kite.

Timmy tries.

Eric flies a kite.

Timmy tries.

Tina   flies   a   kite.

Timmy tries.

Timmy flies a kite!